ENDORSEMENTS

"This book is a powerful testament to the transformative power of personal responsibility and vision. The author not only shares his remarkable journey from adversity to success, but also provides a compelling blueprint for anyone looking to reshape their life. Through practical exercises and profound insights, he guides readers to not only dream of a better future but to actively create it. This book is an essential read for anyone ready to take control of their destiny and achieve the extraordinary. Truly inspiring!"

— Barbara Diaz de Leon,
RN Bestselling Author of "Feel Great in 28"

"'I Can't Doesn't Exist' is one of the most thought provoking, inspiring, insightful, practical, and transformative books I have ever read. This is a major self-help book needed for your personal library. I recommend this book to the world!"

— Tressa Mitchener Bestselling
Author of "Looking Out From the Inside"

"'I Can't Doesn't Exist' is a transformative journey that reminds us of our divine potential. This book beautifully articulates how each of us carries a spark of the divine, empowering us with the ability to shape our reality. Through its compelling narrative, the authors dismantle the deeply ingrained beliefs that limit our success, health, love, and prosperity. The study questions at the end of each chapter are particularly effective, encouraging deep reflection and practical application of the book's principles. This isn't just a book; it's a movement towards unleashing our inherent greatness. Highly recommended for anyone ready to challenge their limits and embrace the boundless possibilities of life."

— Ana Parra Vivas,
Multi-Award-Winning Author,
"I Trust My Inner Voice"

"The pages of this book will provide you with powerful insights into an inspirational life story. Prepare to marvel at the transformational ideas and actionable steps in 'I Can't Doesn't Exist.' You absolutely do not want to miss out on these compelling ideologies and guiding principles!"

— Judy O'Beirn
President of Hasmark Publishing International

I CAN'T DOESN'T EXIST

By
Ross Garcia

Hasmark
PUBLISHING
INTERNATIONAL

Published by
Hasmark Publishing International
www.hasmarkpublishing.com

Disclaimer

This book is designed to provide information and motivation to our readers. It is sold with the understanding that the publisher is not engaged to render any type of medical, psychological, legal, or any other kind of professional advice. The content of each article is the sole expression and opinion of its author, and not necessarily that of the publisher. No warranties or guarantees are expressed or implied by the publisher's choice to include any of the content in this volume. Neither the publisher nor the individual author shall be liable for any physical, psychological, emotional, financial, or commercial damages, including, but not limited to, special, incidental, consequential, or other damages. Our views and rights are the same: You are responsible for your own choices, actions, and results. This book is for educational and informational purposes only. The content of this book should not be interpreted as medical or professional advice. The reader should carefully evaluate the information provided and consult with a licensed health-care professional before making any decisions or taking any actions based on the content of this book. All the information has been checked to the best of our ability to be factually correct at the time of print. New research gets published often.

Permission should be addressed to Ross Garcia at:
wealthmindsetinfo@gmail.com.

Cover Design: Real Visuals Marketing (creative@realvisualsmarketing.com)
Layout Artist: Amit Dey (amit@hasmarkpublishing.com)

ISBN 13: 978-1-77482-266-1
ISBN 10: 1-77482-266-0

DEDICATION

To my dad, Rosendo Garcia López,
whose unwavering support and
love have been my guiding light.

ACKNOWLEDGEMENTS

I want to acknowledge Dan R. Matthews; for without his help, this book would not be possible.

TABLE OF CONTENTS

INTRODUCTION

Hello, everyone. I'm Ross Garcia. I'm finally bringing you a book that I've been thinking about writing for a long time. It came to me one evening during dinner, and I decided to jot it down because I liked the title. I felt the title was so catchy that when people saw it, they'd think, "Hey, this sounds cool." I really wanted to share something cool, connect with you, and make you say, "This is awesome!"

The beautiful part of the journey is when you're working your way up. It's energizing! It's not that way when you're down because then you have to have faith in yourself.

I was never an author, and I never did great in English or literature, but I always said to myself, "I have a story to tell." I could tell somebody something in my way, and it would connect with them.

I realized that this was the most important part: getting the information out so people could understand, take it into their minds and hearts, and apply it to make a difference. I think this message can change lives.

It's easy to tell your own story out loud. The hard part is writing it down. But if you write a little bit at a time for a long time, just a few sentences or a page, eventually you could fill a book. Then I thought, "Why don't I just talk about my life?" Talking is easy for me. I can simply recount my past, my journey, and my life as it happened. I can just make a series of recordings, sharing my thoughts, and then transcribe them. This is my way of presenting my book—by talking to you and collaborating with various individuals on this journey.

That doesn't mean it was easy. It wasn't easy, because when you want something that is way over the top, it's very difficult. It requires navigating numerous barriers, overcoming obstacles, and clearing fences one after another. You might even feel like you're going through barbed wire, getting scratched up in the process. But the crucial aspect is not to stay in that situation. The key is progression—moving through barriers, circumventing obstacles, and advancing to the next level.

The title of the book is *I Can't Doesn't Exist*. We'll explore each chapter, and after reading this book several times, you might find yourself saying, **"I can exists!"**

In almost everyone's life, "I can't" does exist. This is true because everything in your life is actually in your mind. We'll talk more about that later.

We're embarking on this journey, tapping into different areas of your mind that you may not have known existed before. You'll discover that "I can't" is often something imposed on you by someone else in your life who said, "You can't" or "You can't do it right." This reminds me of Nike's slogan, "Just do it."

Chapter 1

WHO SAID YOU CAN'T?

T he first chapter of *I Can't Doesn't Exist* is here!

The first chapter is titled "Who Said You Can't?"

Now, here's where you need to start really thinking deeply. Engage your memory. Begin by revisiting your past, particularly when you were a child. Recall moments when you were eager to buy something, and people were quick to say, "Well, you know you can't afford it. You don't have enough money. You can't buy that!" How many times were you told you "can't"—whether at work, in a relationship, at school, or by your parents, cousins, or loved ones? They said:

- "You can't do it!"
- "That's not right!"
- "You can't ask for more money at your job!"
- "You can't buy a car!"

- "You can't retire young!"
- "You can't have a relationship!"
- "You can't be wealthy!"
- "You can't travel the world!"

What they are essentially saying to you is, "Let's just focus more on the negative."

Okay, sure. Let's focus more on why you supposedly can't. Okay. Let's go into detail about why you can't. Perhaps it's because you didn't go to school, or you're considered a minority—a statistic. Maybe it's because you weren't raised in a productive family. Maybe you "can't" because you lack the funds to buy a car or you've never had a stable relationship. Perhaps you can't because you're not an author, you didn't attend school, and your grades weren't stellar.

Alright. You dropped out of school before graduating. Maybe you even dropped out in 8th grade and never attended high school. Maybe you can't travel because it wasn't a norm in your family, or the best job you had was at McDonald's. Maybe you can't because you struggle to focus or concentrate—you're perceived as an idiot, right? Not a nice word, but it's thrown around. Maybe you can't because no one in your family has ever done it, so why should you try?

So, you can't. Maybe it's because you're not good enough. Maybe you're just not a leader; maybe you're just not productive. Maybe you don't clean your house or go to the gym. Maybe you look like shit (excuse my language). Maybe you can't because all the odds seem against you, so why bother? Why would you be capable of achieving it?

But who actually said you can't?

Let's think about that. Who said it? It was everyone in your life. You can't because they couldn't. However, when you heard everyone saying, "You can't," suddenly you started saying, "I can't." Once you began believing what others said, that's where you went wrong, because there's more of them than you.

And they're all saying the same thing: "You can't." Why? Because of one thing—it's all they know about their own lives! Even though they're mistaken, there's only one you, but there's a lot of them.

Think of a sports event. There may be hundreds or thousands of people watching a basketball game, but there are only 10 players on the court. Thousands in the audience have conflicting beliefs—half think one team can't win, and the other half believes the opposite!

Do the players listen to those doubting voices? No! They give their best, listening to their coach and those on their side.

This scenario mirrors your own life. You may encounter a thousand people telling you that you can't do something. Don't listen to them. Just do your best.

Similarly, within our minds, two sides of thinking coexist—logic and fantasy. Society conditions us to think like everyone else. Logically, you might hear one side saying, "You can't," because everyone else said so, and from the beginning, you echo, "I can't." So you remain stuck, unable to change or get ahead because you lent an ear to that voice of doubt.

But here's the promise: things are about to change for you!

This book is here to guide you out of this situation so that you can confidently say, "I can!" because YOU CAN! I can. Everyone can.

The saying goes, "Where there's a will, there's a way." Your will is your ability to focus on one thought without distraction.

Remember how you focused the first time you fell in love? You couldn't focus on anything else. Just do it!

Direct your focus toward that will. Why is it said that where there's a will, there's a way? When you focus the will, you employ a higher faculty—an intellectual faculty. It's a God-given ability.

You have higher faculties, including:

- imagination
- will
- reasoning

- intuition
- memory
- perception

When you engage the higher faculties, you can tap into a world that was erased from your mind—erased by teachers, society, the matrix that whispered, "You can't!"

Perhaps you were told you could sell cars but never drive them, that you could sell cars but never own the lot or run a business, because "You just can't." You're deemed too stupid, too dumb.

Maybe it wasn't your teacher; it could have been a friend when you had an aspiration to say, "Hey! You know I want to be successful," only to be kicked in the butt by family and friends.

And what did you say? What did you do? You repeated, "I can't," and for 20 years, you lived saying, "It's not possible. I can't do it." But your life doesn't have to be that way!

People often reach out to me, saying things like,

"I just don't have any money."

Or

"I can't do it well."

I respond with suggestions like, "Why don't you meet me in Barcelona?"

"I can't. I don't have the money to go to Europe."

"Then why don't you meet me in Chicago?"

"I can't. I don't have the money to go to Chicago."

Let's focus on what's happening here. You're busy using your lower faculties—your analytical mind that relies on seeing, smelling, tasting, hearing, and touching, which is easy; that's easy.

Everyone does that.

You're not concentrating on your will. However, there is a will, and it's operated by your higher faculties. That is your true will, and it can take you where you thought you couldn't go.

Understand that everyone will tell you what they feel, but you know what? They don't know because they gave up on themselves long ago. They stopped trying; some even stopped thinking! That's why 1% of people own most businesses and make the majority of the money.

This book centers on time, money, change, and freedom. If you convince yourself that you can't, then you can't. You think you can't, and you're right. You fabricate reasons why you can't—no time, no money, lacking experience or education, missing the right elements. You talk yourself into a hole by telling yourself lies. You desire freedom, and to achieve it, you must understand that you can't have it if you believe you can't. You can't have it because you need to have time, money, or freedom. Freedom to travel the world when you please; money that makes more money; and ideas that will bring you multiple sources of income now.

"I can't" may seem like mere words, but a word is very powerful—it can reshape your thinking. Focusing on those words builds an image in your mind of why you can't, and you'll start seeing yourself as a lesser person on this planet.

The reality is that you are a heavenly spirit living in a human body, here to fulfill a higher purpose. You're meant to focus on what you want to do, and slowly, you'll get there, saying, "I can!"

Sure, there are stumbling blocks, obstacles, and walls in your way, but none of them can stop you unless you think, "I can't."

"I can't" is a brick wall. "I can" helps you break through that wall. This book, through repetition, will help you break down that wall.

You'll encounter doubts, and you'll once again think, "I can't." And you'll be right unless you do one thing—make a **decision** to change.

This book is here to help you break limitations and to break through the "Terror Barrier," the mental brick wall, the daunting obstacle that's only real in your mind—but is terrifying.

This book is designed to assist you in reaching the next level, to make a quantum leap in your time, money, and freedom. So, who really said, "You can't"? It was you, not the thousands who don't understand. Right now, you believe them, but that will change, and you will start believing the truth. You CAN.

William James, a professor at Harvard University in the 1900s, imparted a profound insight:

"Believe in your belief, and your belief will literally create the fact."

Believe in your belief. Consider what you've believed in until now—it's likely been *their* beliefs, and *their* beliefs come with limitations, often starting with "I can't."

"I can't," "you can't," and "they couldn't" became a cycle that kept you stuck. Let's break free from that!

Let's shift our focus to why—all the reasons *you can*:

- be successful
- be great
- be intelligent
- create something from nothing
- travel the world
- make more money
- have residual income
- have more stable sources of income

You *can*. We're going to construct images of why you can, and you will stay there. These images will manifest into physical form through your mind.

You can!

Chapter 1 Study Questions

1. Write about the time you started on your journey of discovering yourself and your purpose in life.

_____

_____

_____

_____

_____

2. In the early days of your journey, what were some of the barriers you faced that kept you from moving forward?

_____

_____

_____

_____

_____

3. What were some of the "I can't" beliefs you learned as a child? Who shaped them?

_____

_____

_____

_____

_____

4. What do you want most in life? Write down what you
   would really love if money were not an issue and you
   could not fail.

   _____

   _____

   _____

   _____

   _____

Chapter 2

YOU VERSUS YOU

I t's no one else.

It has always been you versus you.

You've been telling yourself these things.

You've been focusing on yourself, and why yourself?

You know how the dialogue unfolds between those voices in your head. It's something like this:

"You can't."

or

"Why you?"

or

"Who do you think you are?"

or

"You don't know how."

The voice tells you:

- why you couldn't
- why you believed it
- why it's unfair
- why you don't have enough of this or enough of that

Why is it you versus you, and not you versus *them*? Because *they* are not in control of your life. And *they* do not live with you.

Only you live with you.

Only you wake up to you.

Only you can make the decision to get up and go to the gym, engage in something productive, or go for a walk. Only you decide to invest your time in something beneficial or to nurture positive and creative thoughts.

Only you possess the ability to think for yourself.

No one else could ever think for you, so the battle of you versus you is a clash between you, the master, and you, the victim.

Who will emerge victorious? I'll tell you. It's not a mystery. Winning is determined by law.

The version of you that triumphs is the one to which you devote the most attention.

Let's master the part of you that tends to be the victim. Let's focus on how many thoughts you have throughout the day and what they are. I'll show you how.

Let's get rid of the "I can't" because it doesn't exist.

It never did.

It only "existed" in your mind, shaped by an image you entertained throughout the day, and all that contemplation shaped your reality. Your thinking created your world.

This is why what you perceive through your lower faculty, guided by your reasoning mind, doesn't look right. It's not appealing. What you see is something not right, so let's deliberately divert attention away from what doesn't look right. Direct your focus solely toward what you like and what you are capable of, disregarding the limitations imposed by others or the ones you imposed on yourself.

You can do anything you want.

However, if you focus on "I can't," then "I can't" will coexist alongside "I can."

Which one wins is up to you.

Only entertain the notion of "I can."

You can, and this ability comes from the power within you.

The authority of "I can" or "I can't" is granted life through your belief in it.

So, let's breathe life into "I can." Okay? Let's master YOU. How do you master you? It's done by KNOWING what you love—what you really, really love.

What does that mean? It means you must harbor a burning desire for something, something you have to create from nothing. When you focus on what you love with the thought of "I can," you are essentially creating something out of nothing.

Recognize that we exist in two realms: the physical and the spiritual. The spiritual world, at times, may seem like a fantastical realm. However, it is undeniably real because, in the subconscious mind, all possible realities exist.

Begin contemplating the reality you desire and direct your focused attention toward it. Add to that the burning desire of what you really, really want. Your emotions will infuse your focused attention with additional energy, acting as fuel for the burning desire.

I recall joining Bob Proctor's company in 2016 when they informed me about an upcoming event in New York named the Modern-Day Millionaire. A friend of Bob Proctor was hosting the event at the prestigious Carnegie Hall.

Carnegie Hall! Built with a significant donation from Andrew Carnegie. For those unfamiliar with Andrew Carnegie, he was a highly successful steel manufacturer in the late 1800s and early 1900s.

Carnegie held the title of the richest person in the United States.

In 1905, he crossed paths with a young newspaper reporter named Napoleon Hill.

Napoleon Hill was the author of the bestselling book on success, *Think and Grow Rich*, along with works like *The Laws of Success*, *Outwitting the Devil*, and *How to Raise Your Own Salary*. When the two met, Carnegie proposed, "Would you like to write about the laws of success to help the modern man?" Napoleon Hill took about 28 seconds to respond, stating, "Yes, Mr. Carnegie, sir, you can depend on me. I will achieve it."

What does this narrative have to do with the notion that "I Can't Doesn't Exist?" Until that moment, Napoleon Hill grappled with his own limitations. He was unfamiliar with the concept of philosophy, lacked knowledge about book writing, possessed no financial means, and had no connections with wealthy and successful people.

However, Andrew Carnegie reassured him, affirming, "You can do it, starting now."

Here I am, an ordinary individual raised amid limitations and trained to perceive life through the lens of "I can't."

Yet, here I sit, in Carnegie Hall, listening as my mentor, Bob Proctor, recounts the tale of Andrew Carnegie and Napoleon Hill's encounter in New York. It's my first time in this esteemed venue.

Amid the beautiful red seats, surrounded by famous people, I look at the top rows and see Les Brown. Facing toward me is Bob Proctor, as Sandy Gallagher walks with him on stage.

At that moment, as I look at my mentor standing on stage before me armed with two pieces of paper, he recounts the tale of how Napoleon Hill met Andrew Carnegie in the 1900s. Bob Proctor noted that if it weren't for Andrew Carnegie, *Think and Grow Rich* wouldn't exist.

But let's return to the point. Napoleon Hill grappled with many limitations. His mind became a battleground, haunted by the echoes of people from his past who harbored the "I can't" mentality. For a few seconds, he thought, "I can't," but then he decided that he could. He decided to take the leap, declaring, "Yes, sir." He boarded a train to interview Andrew Carnegie, spending all his money to get there. He didn't even have enough money to get back home.

As a young newspaper reporter, Napoleon Hill gambled everything to interview Andrew Carnegie. Fortunately,

Andrew Carnegie saw something in Napoleon Hill that Hill didn't see in himself. Carnegie observed that Hill made decisions quickly and had a certainty. He knew that Hill would go the extra mile.

Andres Carnegie recognized the potential for greatness. That's what a mentor does.

A mentor sees something in his or her student that the student can't see in themself. Andrew Carnegie recognized this potential in Napoleon Hill and asked him, "Would you like to talk about the laws of success?"

To this, Napoleon answered immediately, "Yes, Mr. Carnegie. sir. You can depend on me. I will achieve it."

Napoleon Hill spent the next three days at Andrew Carnegie's mansion. During this time, they planned the trajectory of Napoleon Hill's life for the next 25 years. His mission: to interview over 500 of the wealthiest people in the world, unraveling the common threads that bound their success. Then, he was to write a book. The rest, as they say, is history.

Fast forward to my reality, seated in New York, listening intently to Bob Proctor. I had never set foot in New York before, never seen the Statue of Liberty with my own eyes. But here I am in the audience, absorbing the narrative of how Napoleon Hill crossed paths with Andrew Carnegie.

It's a battle—You versus You.

It's you versus you; it's not you versus them.

You believed "I can't" before.

But you can. I could. I did. I do. I've done it.

In New York, I witnessed Bob Proctor's wisdom first-hand. I shook his hand and told him, "I work with your company."

"Congratulations! I'm happy for you," responded Bob.

My focus now centers on writing books. It's you versus you.

Think about how many times you've told yourself something isn't possible. You said:

"I can't make $1,000,000."

or

"I can't open a business."

But you can.

Seated in Carnegie Hall, Bob Proctor recounted Andrew Carnegie's directive to Napoleon Hill. Carnegie said, "I know you can't do this now. But you will be able to do it, if and only if you believe you can do it. I want you to look yourself in the mirror, Napoleon, and tell yourself, 'Andrew Carnegie, I'm going to surpass your achievements. I'm going to meet you at the post and pass you at the Grandstand!'"

Napoleon, initially hesitant, replied, "Mr. Carnegie, you're the richest person in the world. There's no way that I could look in the mirror and tell myself a lie."

Carnegie insisted that he could if he believed he could. He tasked Hill with daily affirmations of "I can" in front of the mirror until belief took root. And so, Napoleon Hill complied.

Remember, it's you versus you.

Up to this point, at Carnegie Hall, my life was a disaster—a complete disaster.

Maybe you, too, feel like your life is a disaster.

What I want you to do is to look in the mirror just like Andrew Carnegie told Napoleon Hill to do. Peer into that reflective surface, and declare to yourself something profound; tell yourself what you really love. Then say, "I can do it. I know that 'I can' does exist, and I will do it, and I'm doing it right now."

Understand that it's you versus you. Stand up to yourself.

The past, the present, and the future are already done, so how do we move toward the future with our past thinking? How do we conquer ourselves in our own minds?

By thinking productively.

Think "I can" and "Anything is possible."

I want to give you this lesson. Look at yourself in the mirror. It's you versus you. Acknowledge that up to this point, you've been the one telling yourself that you couldn't do it. It's not "them" who convinced you. They may have told you, "You can't do it," but you're the one who believed it.

I want you to understand. I want you to believe in yourself, and I want you to believe in the person in the mirror. Stop arguing with that person. Stop fighting with that person in the mirror, because arguing with yourself won't produce results.

It's you versus you.

I embraced the challenge of facing myself in the mirror, telling myself that I am a productive author, a New York Times bestseller, and an Amazon bestseller. I am actively working toward that goal by delivering this information to you. I not only know it, but I also believe it. If you don't believe it yet, at least believe that I do.

Remember the wisdom of William James:

"Believe in your belief, and your belief will literally create the fact."

Chapter 2 Study Questions

1. Give four examples of your own inner conversations with the voice of "I can't." What reasons did you give yourself?

    _____

    _____

    _____

    _____

    _____

2. Which voice are you giving the most attention to: the voice of "I can" or the voice of "I can't"? Explain why.

    _____

    _____

    _____

    _____

    _____

3. Give an example of how your thinking has created the world you live in.

    _____

    _____

    _____

    _____

    _____

4. Write an "I can" statement to yourself. Next, find a mirror and repeat it to yourself with passion and emotion. Do this 10 times.

_____

_____

_____

_____

_____

Chapter 3

LIMITATIONS

Everyone believes in limits.

People commonly think there's a limit to how much wealth one can accumulate, how deep true love can be, how healthy they can be, and in other parts of life. They harbor beliefs that:

- There's a limit on how swiftly progress can happen.
- There's a limit to how much money you can make.
- There's a boundary to the available time.
- There are limits to virtually every conceivable aspect of life.

But the reality is, there is no limit.

The only limits that exist are the ones you adopt as truth. Once accepted by you, these limits become your reality.

Napoleon Hill astutely observed that the only limit that ever existed is the one constructed within your own mind. Your mind possesses such incredible power that you can literally tap into anything you want.

Every element in the world resonates with its own unique energy or frequency, akin to a cell phone number. Your thoughts operate in vibrations manifested as images or emotions. The mental images you're entertaining or concentrating on are the architects of your external reality.

Don't look at the outside world and simply let it entertain you. You've created it. Draw it close to you and embrace it.

Understand that if you believe in the possibility of "I can't," you create the circumstances that make that statement true.

Know that you can be productive and make things happen with a few key steps.

Firstly, BELIEVE that you can. There are no limitations. As Napoleon Hill puts it, "The only limitation that exists is the one that exists in your own mind."

Everything—possibilities, achievements, barriers— already existed in your thinking before it existed in the physical realm.

When you admire the Mona Lisa painting, you're not seeing the original; it left when Leonardo da Vinci died.

What you see is a replica, a second copy. The original, the first copy, existed in his mind. Consider this when observing art.

Likewise, think about that when you're looking at your current results. To transition from "I can't" to "I can," shift your thinking, alter your beliefs, and understand that there is no limit to the levels you can reach.

Reflecting on my journey, I remember making my first $2,000,000. It took considerable time and a lot of hard work. Progressing from 2 million to 50 million presented a significant mental stretch, but I accomplished it more swiftly than the initial 2 million. Reaching 50 million filled me with excitement.

Yet Wallace Wattles, in *The Science of Getting Rich*, advises against excitement. Instead, view it as a part of your growing process. Expect it and accept it with gratitude.

There is absolutely no limit. Just as I progressed from 50 million to 100 million, the potential exists to reach a billion. Similarly, you can achieve 100,000 dollars, a million, or 10 million. Your belief system dictates the outcome without limitations.

Focus on the detailed picture of what you love, homing in on each aspect. You have to focus clearly on the positive emotions associated with success, experiencing the joy of already having achieved it.

Psychologists note that we generate approximately 60,000 thoughts per day, with only about 2% related to what we really want, what we desire. The rest are minor, fear-driven, or limiting thoughts.

Analyze these thoughts as they come in, as they are often shaped by external influences, such as television, social media, friends, or family, dictating your results. It's forcing the opinions of the outside world into your mind.

Instead of allowing these thoughts to percolate, seek solace in a quiet place. Read books that reinforce the "I can" mentality, countering the feeling of "I can't" and dispelling limitations imposed by those who said, "You can't do it."

Believe that there are no limits; the only boundary exists in your mind.

The things you desire are already within you, existing on a particular frequency and vibration. Connecting your subconscious mind with the strong emotional feelings associated with the thought of having achieved your goal.

Your sense of accomplishment further opens your subconscious mind, giving energy to the feeling of "I can."

Emotion fuels the fire of your burning desire, intensifying the shift from "I can't" to "I can."

If you don't feel positive about your goal, attracting the things you desire becomes challenging. Embrace a sense of amazement about it, because you deserve it. There are no limits.

When I imagine a life without limits, I think about flying cars. Consider the movie *The Fifth Element* with Bruce Willis as the character Korben Dallas. In the film, Korben drives a flying taxi. In one scene, a woman rushes onto the screen. She turns out to be Korben's love interest by the movie's end, and in a way, love becomes the savior of both her and the world.

In a pivotal moment, she jumps into the taxi. "Help me!" she shouts to Korben. "Help me!" The police, in hot pursuit, are unaware of her identity. Shots are fired at Korben's flying taxi in the skies of New York City. Nearby, a Chinese man casually prepares food, and people are floating in the sky like *The Jetsons*. This scene, typical of sci-fi movies like *Star Wars*, highlights the incredible power of thought and imagination to create worlds without limits.

I want you to consider a world without limits. Envision flying cars, and embrace the idea that all realities are within reach. Imagine tapping into any image from the fantastical depths of books—dive down the rabbit hole. These may seem like fantasies, but so were the communicators in *Star Trek*. But this has now become a reality with cell phones. Fantasy became reality.

Embrace the idea that what you would really love in your life is within reach at this very moment. Of course, you have to keep your common sense—gravity still exists. If you jump out a window, you're not going to fly like Superman.

What I'm telling you is that your thinking has been shaped by societal programming since childhood. Recognizing this will make you aware of where your thoughts are coming from, allowing you to filter and alter those that hold you back.

You've been confined to a world that preached "you can't." You stayed there, but you don't need to stay there any longer. Once you understand, you have power. It's time to break free from the matrix and liberate yourself from the influence of other people's opinions of what's possible.

Breaking free might seem daunting, especially when this has been your only reality. How do you do it?

How can you break free when this is the only world you have ever known? Just remember, the world you are trying to change is yours!

It's your world.

With this information, I'm crafting a vivid image in your mind. Like the flying car. You need to understand—there are no limitations. None. You can go as far as you want to go. With the power of your mind and imagination, you can traverse galaxies, just like the Jedis in *Star Wars*, exploring new worlds.

You, too, can explore new worlds, and they can become real thanks to the power of your thoughts.

In your quest to flee from the Empire, you find that the Empire strikes back. It relentlessly seeks to eliminate the true you. It's a never-ending battle between good and evil, between positive and negative forces, and you are an integral part of this struggle.

It's important to acknowledge that maintaining a consistently positive mindset may not always be feasible. And that's okay. What matters is that you understand that anything that you think consistently is creating your reality around you.

Flying cars might only exist in the realm of our imaginations, but if enough people collectively envision them, we could all be flying soon. It will happen in time.

So where does that leave us? We have some limitations, but we also have the ability to focus on the infinite possibilities.

Choose to focus on the notion that anything's possible. "I can" exists. Because "I can" does exist.

Tell yourself, "I'm not going to believe them. I'm going to believe in myself. I'm going to create my own reality."

Tell yourself, "I'm going to stop talking about all the reasons why I can't. I'm only talking about the reasons why I can, and better yet, I've already done it!"

Understand that energy is neither created nor destroyed, and everything that exists is already here. It's already done. Any new idea you have has already existed in the infinite universe of ideas. But when it comes to you, it can be materialized in your real world.

How and when it comes into existence hinges on the limitations you place on yourself. Get rid of your own limitations to make room for the creation of what you imagine.

Chapter 3 Study Questions

1. What do you believe is holding you back from success? Where is that belief coming from?

_____

_____

_____

_____

_____

2. Based on your answer to #1, why do you allow this belief to control your ability to succeed? What can you do to change it?

_____

_____

_____

_____

_____

3. Imagine the life you would love to live. Describe that perfect life in complete detail.

_____

_____

_____

_____

_____

4. Describe how your elevated emotions can help you to achieve your goal. Think of the emotions you have in your perfect life.

_____

_____

_____

_____

_____

Chapter 4

SAY IT AGAIN: "I CAN!"

S ay it: "I can!"

Say it again, "I can exist! I can do this! I can create whatever I want!" The more you affirm "I can," the more you are going to change the outside world.

When you say, "I can," you may want to write down the specifics. Why can you do this? Because anything is possible. Because nothing is created or destroyed; everything you want is already here. Because:

- "I have higher faculties."
- "I have my imagination."
- "I have concentration; my will."
- "I can focus on my imagination."
- "I can focus on the image of what I really love."

"I can use my God-given abilities to tap into another dimension of success. I can show them that 'I can' and that 'I did it,' and that this is the new me. This is who I am. This is what I'm creating, and they'll see the fruits. They'll see the harvest."

So, say, "I can! I can! I can!"

When I look around, I see what appears to be a real world. But I would describe it like this: nothing is real.

Reality is shaped by your perception and belief system. Wallace Wattles, in *The Science of Getting Rich*, talks about a 'thinking stuff' that fills everything from which all things are made. A thought impressed upon this substance manifests the imagined thing. This thinking substance encompasses all space and time, often referred to as the eternal NOW.

When you observe the world through your eyesight, one of the lower physical faculties, you may see a pen or a piece of paper. But is it truly a pen? Is it genuinely a piece of paper?

Examining it through your higher intellectual faculties reveals that it's made of a lot of different things. Paper is comprised of tiny cellulose fibers, which are made of molecules, themselves constructed of atoms like carbon, hydrogen, and oxygen. These atoms consist of subatomic particles, such as electrons and protons, each vibrating at its own frequency and exchanging information with other particles. They are in constant communication.

However, you may not be aware of these intricate levels of vibration unless you engage your higher intellectual faculties, such as intuition, imagination, and reason. Recognize that there are laws you apply in your daily life in the so-called real world, and there are other laws that often go unused.

This chapter delves into uncovering the hidden laws often overlooked, allowing you to understand what they are. While you share sensory experiences like seeing, smelling, tasting, hearing, and touching—so can a dog. Likewise, a dog may excel in certain lower faculties, such as smell. But you were not born with the limitations of a dog.

You also possess reason, will, imagination, intuition, memory, perception, and a self-image. These intellectual faculties are far more advanced than those of animals, enabling you to understand who you are. You comprehend "I AM," a concept foreign to a dog.

Now, as we navigate through this chapter, it's essential to stay engaged, even if things seem confusing. Numerous laws govern the natural world, known as physical or scientific laws.

Simultaneously, there exist other laws controlling not only the physical realm but also the unseen or spiritual world, such as:

- the laws that control the creation process

- the law of transmutation or change of energy
- the law of vibration
- the law of rhythm
- the law of cause and effect
- and many more!

We'll explore these laws and more in the next book, but I want you to understand that what you perceive as real is real in one sense, but at the same time, it is not real at the same level.

To become a millionaire or billionaire, you must adopt the mindset of one. Envision yourself in that role, affirming, "I can do it! I can do it!" and eradicating the notion that "I can't" exists.

Reality, in one sense, emerges from your thinking.

Remember: 'thinking stuff' forms the basis of all things, and thoughts impressed upon this stuff create the thing imagined by the thought.

You are at the center of this creative process, the driver of the vehicle. Your thoughts mold tangible things from the invisible energy of thought. While this thinking stuff remains unseen, your perception shapes what you consider real.

Entering different mental landscapes, akin to movies like *Alice in Wonderland* or *The Matrix*, reveals that what seems real on one level may not hold the same truth on another. The world around you isn't inherently real; it is made real through your belief in its reality.

You observe people filling their cars with gasoline, wondering about the concerns over gas prices and the queues at gas stations. The reality they experience is one they've collectively created. Witnessing others use gasoline for their vehicles, they find themselves needing it to drive. Do we truly need gasoline to propel a vehicle?

These are the questions you should be asking yourself about what is genuinely necessary in your world. Do you need to follow a conventional path to wealth? Do you need to remain where you are right now? The concept of wealth is crafted in your mind.

"You can't paint the kitchen by painting the outside of the house."

As my mentor, Bob Proctor, often emphasized: to paint the kitchen, you must begin with the kitchen before moving on to other rooms.

Similarly, analyzing your life from within, understanding your current state, is the starting point for creating your reality.

The thinking stuff, as mentioned, gains power through repetition. By consistently focusing on the things you desire, you send potent thoughts to your subconscious mind. From there, your subconscious mind shapes the reality you spend the most time contemplating.

Stop relying solely on the lower physical faculties—sight, smell, taste, hearing, and touch. If you only use your lower faculties, you will only get the same results. When you let the outside world dictate your thoughts, you perpetuate the same results. As Wallace Wattles asks in *The Science of Getting Rich*, "What is real?"

In this journey of life, you are a spiritual being having a human experience, aiming to understand what is real. Learning from life's lessons, striving to ascend from the bottom to the top. But to do that, you have to know what the top looks like. Visualize the end result in your life, and more importantly, immerse yourself in the emotions of already being that person, because that's what's going to shape your reality.

According to William James, the first professor of American psychology, an individual entertains around 40 to 60 thousand thoughts per day—thoughts about what they want and what they don't want. This fact is crucial to remember.

Recall the law of polarity, which coexists with the law of transmutation of energy (or the law of vibration and attraction). Positive and negative thoughts operate under the law of polarity. Throughout the day, these 60,000 thoughts, governed by the laws, influence your results.

Yet, as you observe your life through your eyesight and define your world based on your physical senses, you perpetuate the same life you've already been living.

Take command of those 60,000 thoughts using your higher faculties, by wielding your will. This enables you to imprint a powerful image on your subconscious mind, crafting the reality of the world you would love to see.

Stop looking at the reality you wish to avoid. Embrace what truly is real. Stop and think. Try meditating in a quiet spot in your house. This practice will help you control and focus your thoughts, and this will help you create your new world.

I admire Thomas Edison. He used to take cat naps during the day, entering a dream world where he envisioned new solutions and things he wanted to see. He claimed to have gone through 10,000 failures before eventually succeeding in creating the incandescent lightbulb. During one of these cat naps, he conceived the idea of sending sound as a frequency. This led to the invention of the phonograph.

In the realm of thought, our reality operates on different channels, each representing a unique frequency. Your attention determines the channel or reality you inhabit. Amid the billions of other channels, different frequencies dictate different realities or dimensions. There are numerous channels.

Focus on the frequency of the thought aligned with what you truly love, the special channel for you, and send that image to your subconscious mind—the part of you controlling your vibration. By concentrating on this thought, you can start to create your own reality.

Stop fixating on the reality of your past. Stop letting it control the way you think. We deal with the now, the end result. Adopt the actor's technique of assuming a new role. Take the Marlon Brando approach to acting—assume the role of the new YOU.

You must play the leading role in your life.

Does it really exist in your own mind? Does being broke truly exist in your mind's portrayal of your perfect new life? Or are you progressing to a chapter marked by a quantum leap in your income?

Chapter 4 Study Questions

1. Anything is possible! Without limiting yourself, write down four "I CAN!" statements that describe how amazing you are.

_____

_____

_____

_____

_____

2. What makes your world real? List some of the perceptions or beliefs that have created the world you live in now.

_____

_____

_____

_____

_____

3. How much money do you want to make? By what date do you want to earn it? What will you do to make it? Write it all down.

_____

_____

_____

_____

_____

4. Go into a quiet place in your home. Sit in a chair. Close your eyes and take a deep breath. Now, imagine you have the money you want. Imagine your life in detail for 10 minutes. Then, write down the words that describe the wonderful emotions you feel.

_____

_____

_____

_____

_____

Chapter 5

THE OUTSIDE WORLD

The outside world is what's telling you, "I can't does exist." It insists, "You can't do it. There's no way it can be done. No one has ever done it before."

Throughout the history of sports, there had never been a person who could run a mile in less than four minutes. However, in 1954, a college athlete shattered this perceived "barrier" that no one ever thought would be broken. Roger Bannister, driven by an unwavering belief in his ability, focused relentlessly on this seemingly impossible goal. Despite the skepticism of experts who claimed it couldn't be done, Roger persisted. He not only broke the barrier but also paved the way for more runners to realize they could achieve it, too. Astonishingly, Roger's record was broken after a mere two months. Today, over 1700 individuals, ranging from 17 to over 40 years old, have conquered the mile in under four minutes. What was once only conceivable for Roger became a reality for countless others.

Suddenly, there was a surge of runners achieving sub-four-minute miles, as if a floodgate had been opened by someone who dared to prove the experts wrong. Breaking such barriers has a profound effect, not only in the physical realm but in the realms of the mind and reality. For barrier-breakers, here's what happens: the creation of something in the mind creates reality in the real world.

There are two types of creation. The first is synthetic creation, where things that already exist are ingeniously combined in novel ways.

Then there's true creation.

True creation happens when you bring something into existence from nothing, setting an example for others that it is indeed possible. The belief that something is not possible, for any number of reasons, constitutes your paradigm. Those who deemed the four-minute mile an insurmountable barrier held a paradigm that made it impossible to conceive as achievable. The phrase "I can't" encapsulates this limiting paradigm.

To break through any paradigm, you must be the trailblazer—whether in your family, your town, or on a global scale. Consider Steve Jobs, who was a trailblazer in the world of smartphones. He thought, "I can!" He dedicated himself to the task, proving it could be accomplished. Once Jobs succeeded, others followed suit, creating other versions of smartphones.

Long before Steve Jobs, there was Thomas Edison. He thought, "I can!" He showed that the incandescent light was possible after failing 10,000 times. He knew it was possible. Why? Because he thought of it.

Edison and Nikola Tesla collaborated when Tesla worked for Edison. Together, they aimed to devise the most efficient electric power generator. A disagreement arose over alternating current (Tesla's preference) versus direct current (Edison's choice). Tesla's approach turned out to be correct, leading to the prevalence of alternating current today. Despite Tesla's triumph, Edison, a prolific inventor with over 400 creations, including the record player and motion picture camera, garnered more fame for his contributions.

Nikola Tesla's popularity is still quite high, evidenced by the naming of the most admired electric car. However, it raises an intriguing question: do we really need electricity to power a vehicle, or could they potentially navigate through the unseen ether?

Remember that if one person can achieve something, it means anyone has the potential to do it. The difference between you and everyone else is that you possess a new understanding—the "I CAN!" attitude. This mindset is also what many religious people refer to as faith. Faith that "I am able!" It's not just about your capabilities but recognizing that, as a child of infinite intelligence, you are connected to boundless possibilities.

What I'm getting at is the world around us, much like Wallace Wattles describes: "There is the thinking stuff from which all things are made. A thought impressed upon this stuff produces the thing that is imaged by the thought..." Whose thought? Yours. Your thoughts shape something from nothing, emerging from the infinite, the quantum field, and boundless energy. You pick just one idea from those 60,000 thoughts, and that single idea has the power to change your outside world.

Why? Because "I can't" does not exist. It's solely a matter of your belief, your evolving understanding, and the universal laws.

Understand that man didn't write these laws.

These laws are above man.

What are the laws? There are many that hold true in both the physical and unseen realms. The law of transmutation of energy, the law of vibration, the law of rhythm, the law of cause and effect, the law of polarity, and finally, the seventh law—the law of gender. Wallace Wattles talks about these laws.

But then you also have the higher faculties:

- **Imagination**: where things are created by thought alone.
- **Will**: your ability to concentrate or focus on just one of those 60 thousand thoughts.
- **Reasoning**: determining relationships between ideas.
- **Intuition**: the sixth sense, when you just know it's true.
- **Memory**: learning from the lessons of the past.
- **Perception**: how you see things at any level.

With intuition, you experience a hunch—an inner feeling that "This is the right thing to do." Recall how Thomas Edison faced challenges in creating the incandescent light-bulb. The idea came to him suddenly through intuition. That's why, in cartoons, for example, we often see light-bulbs over someone's head when they have a great idea.

How did Edison do it? By taking catnaps during the day, he allowed thoughts to come to him. Through this method, he figured out a way to prevent the combustion of the little thread of metal inside the bulb, keeping oxygen outside the bulb and making the metal thread so hot that it glowed. Bingo!

Your outside world exists because you allow it to exist. To control the circumstances and shape your outside world, you must change the way you think.

Once you begin to change the way you think, everything in the outside world will change along with it.

You're going to start writing bigger numbers on your palm. Remember, that's your goal.

To better visualize the bigger number, consider using an index card. Write down the number, and keep the card in your pocket, allowing yourself to feel it and take it out to review during the day. Direct your attention toward it. You might also want to create a goal card stating something like, "I'm so happy and grateful now that I'm making [a definite amount of money] in this area by doing [what you are doing to help others]." Sign and date the goal card for added commitment.

Believe that your plan will manifest because you deserve it, and it certainly will, guided by the law of gender. According to this law, any seed planted will inevitably sprout and grow into a copy of the same plant that produced the seed.

The law of gender parallels the nine-month incubation period for a woman having a child. Similarly, for every seed of thought you sow, you're planting it in your subconscious mind. It's just like planting a corn seed in the ground.

You understand that achieving your goals will take a certain amount of time and require a lot of faith, courage, and
belief. However, once again, the law of gender states that
it will happen. Just as we know the gestation period for
women having a child is nine months, and for plants like
carrots, corn, or potatoes, it's a few days or weeks before
they sprout. We don't, however, have a fixed timeline for
the spiritual seed. The time it takes for a spiritual seed
to sprout can vary—one day or as long as 10 years. It all
depends on your trust in the law and your joy in seeing
that money come in.

In my case, it took about two years. For you, it might be
three. It all depends on the depth of your belief and how
far you're willing to go.

These were just a short summary of the universal laws and
the God-given faculties bestowed upon you and every
other person on Earth. Now, the journey is in your hands.

Chapter 5 Study Questions

1. Your chief aim in life should be something you feel is impossible. Do you think your goal is impossible? Explain why.

   _____

   _____

   _____

   _____

   _____

2. What's the difference between synthetic creation and true creation? Where does true creation come from?

   _____

   _____

   _____

   _____

   _____

3. How is faith described in this chapter? How do you think that faith is related to the notion of "I can!"?

   _____

   _____

   _____

   _____

   _____

4. Write out your goal card like the example in the chapter. Start with "I am so happy..." Write in the present tense and date it.

_____

_____

_____

_____

_____

Chapter 6

AFFIRMATIONS

A n affirmation is a positive statement acknowledging the joy of achieving a goal. It can not only be a positive statement about how you can reach your goal but also why you deserve your goal and how you can help others by reaching it.

Another crucial step is repeating the same affirmation over and over and over again. I repeat it before I go to sleep, and I repeat it when I wake up. With repetition, the subconscious mind becomes a window of opportunity through which you can send the signal of the image of your goal out into the infinite intelligence.

Just like in Napoleon Hill's *Think and Grow Rich* Chapter One. This is your true desire—the thing you genuinely love. Repeating affirmations with emotions sends powerful energy to your subconscious mind.

Recall the affirmation I stated in the previous chapter:

"I'm so happy and grateful now, because money comes to me in increasing quantities through multiple sources on a continuous basis."

You might consider saying this 1000 times throughout the day because, as you say it, you're constructing a clear and powerful mental image. This practice transforms your thoughts into reality, emphasizing the importance of building an image that grows, much like envisioning a penny, then a nickel, followed by a quarter, half a dollar, and eventually a full dollar.

As you expand your mental image, it mirrors the vastness of the expanding universe. It's akin to the rotation of a star and the alignment of all planets.

The presence of planets is a consequence of what we know as gravity, a concept Isaac Newton discovered when observing an apple. Positioned beneath a tree, he realized that both the apple and much heavier objects fall at the same rate, a phenomenon governed by the law of gravity. Gravity is what keeps us grounded.

How can we harness gravity to our advantage in attracting the things we desire? That's the question at hand. Do affirmations play a role? Can we simply tell ourselves:

"I'm so happy and grateful now that my goal of making, having, or doing will arrive by this date____signed by me." Fill in the blanks with your own aspirations and deadlines.

While everyone has a goal and a deadline, 99% might never consider jotting down their goals, an easy practice that often goes overlooked. I can attest to this from personal experience, having seen it happen twice, once with a goal of $1.7 million.

Then, in 2021, it happened once again while I was at a Starbucks in Austria, this time with $120 million. Regrettably, I didn't write it down. The laws, it seems, work the same for everyone, or you could argue that the laws don't work if you don't follow them—depending on your perspective.

I initially wrote the goal of $50 million in my folder, declaring my intent to make that amount in cryptocurrency through a coin called HEX. Surpassing expectations, I actually made $120 million, more than doubling my initial goal.

You can employ the same approach in any area or for any goal you're pursuing. I just happened to find an area that was in need of change. The government's continuous money printing will inevitably lead to the collapse of the dollar. We are on the brink of a shift to digital currencies, whether government-backed crypto digital currencies or an exchange system that grants you control over your own finances.

When that transformation occurs, we won't rely on banks anymore, just like how cell phones have replaced cameras, telephones, and even shopping malls, along with various other devices such as calculators.

We're stepping into another dimension, another world.

Yet, the crucial concept emphasized in this book, *I Can't Doesn't Exist*, is the law of polarity. While "I can't" may exist, it's in the sense that you're crafting your own reality. The law is perpetually in motion, whether you consciously acknowledge it or not.

My reality was set to live off the interest of my cryptocurrency. Your reality might involve opening a clothing line, pursuing a career as a singer or actor, or any other dream you envision. Whatever it is you desire in the world of your dreams, it will expand as long as you keep affirming to yourself, "This is what I'm going to do." It's happened to me twice, and it could happen to you.

Remember, it's easy to overlook this practice. Write down what you want without worrying about how it's going to happen. Focus on what, when, why, and where you want to reach your goal. You don't need to know how. You only need to know why you want this, when you want it, and a notion about where it's going to happen. Again, you don't need to know how.

Be cautious about negative affirmations like, "I'm no good," as this will become your reality. Or statements like,

"I'm going to lose everything," which sets a certain path for losing all you have. Other negative affirmations include:

- I'm an idiot.
- I'm having trouble in school with my homework.
- My mom said I'll never amount to anything.

Check out this story: Thomas Edison actually got kicked out of school just a few weeks into third grade. The principal sent a letter to his mom, claiming that Tom was too stupid for school. However, his mother spun it differently, telling him he could no longer go to school with the other boys because he was too smart. Thanks to this repeated message, Edison grew up believing in his genius. That belief played a pivotal role, and he went on to become a legendary inventor. All because he bought into the idea that he was a genius.

Everything you tell yourself is bound to return, just like a boomerang. It might not circle back immediately, but it will eventually. Take my friend, for instance, when he said, "I want to buy a car." The perpetual wanting persists. Instead, try affirming, "I have a car!"

There's a stark distinction between wanting and having. *Wanting* places you in a state of necessity, while *having* positions you in a state of "It's already accomplished."

So, remember, "I can't" doesn't exist.

It's "I can't" because everything coexists—both "I can't" and "I can." Remember the law of polarity? God separated everything. Man and woman, for example. Opposites abound in our world: hot and cold, up and down, light and dark, wet and dry, raw and cooked. The list goes on.

We live in a world defined by opposites. These opposites provide us with benchmarks, allowing us to gauge our position by comparing and situating ourselves between extremes or poles. Yet, when it comes to "I can't" and "I can," there is no polarity. It's an either-or scenario, much like being in Tahiti or not being in Tahiti. When you affirm your goal, go all in, and success becomes inevitable, by law.

Chapter 6 Study Questions

1. What is an affirmation? What do you need to do so
    that your affirmation can have a positive effect on your
    thinking?

    _____

    _____

    _____

    _____

    _____

2. How many times a day should you repeat your affir-
    mation? Write the number of times you promise to
    repeat yours.

    _____

    _____

    _____

    _____

    _____

3. What four things do you need to know in order to
    reach your goal besides how to write your goal card?

    _____

    _____

    _____

    _____

    _____

4. What does this mean: "There is no polarity between 'I can't' and 'I can'"? Which affirmation do you choose to reach your goal?

_____

_____

_____

_____

_____

Chapter 7

WHAT YOU SEE

What you see is what you get.

However, there's a difference between seeing with your eyes and seeing with your mind. Two worlds coexist—the external and the internal. Remember: each chapter in this book builds on the previous one, aiming to enhance your understanding. Repetition is key for clarity, and over years of teaching and mentoring, I've become very good at explaining.

What you see and understand is:

- who you are
- what you think
- everything that creates your reality

So, what do you see now? This is your moment. Here's a lesson for you:

Write down what you see.

Grab a blank sheet of paper and record your observations. If there's something you dislike, that's fine. Write it down. It's okay to write this now, because we're going to create two papers: one paper with everything that you don't like and another listing everything that you do like.

What we're discussing here has to do with hypnosis. Napoleon Hill referred to this hypnotic process as "auto-suggestion." Where did hypnosis originate?

The term we use today, hypnosis, was once known as *mesmerism*. Where did it come from? The roots of mesmerism can be traced back to Franz Mesmer in 1750. Mesmerism, or as he called it, "animal magnetism," is when you hypnotize somebody.

Some hypnosis practices induce a hypnotic state where individuals experience healing. In this subconscious and hypnotic state, the subconscious mind becomes completely open. Such practices align with what psychologists might employ in therapy sessions.

But you can do this yourself. If you aim to hypnotize yourself using these methods, your goal is to delve into your own thoughts, examine what you see in your mind, and actively change what you see if it isn't serving you. This includes addressing negative thoughts, self-limiting beliefs about yourself, or the sense of being a powerless victim.

You want to write down everything that you don't like about yourself, your limiting beliefs, such as:

- I'm a loser.
- I'm no good.
- I can't do it.
- I can't buy a car.
- I can't buy a house.
- I can't get a job.
- I can't, I can't, I can't…

Take some time to write down a full page of self-limiting beliefs. Following this, grab a piece of fresh paper. For each negative statement you wrote on the initial sheet, counter it by crafting an opposing affirmation, articulating the reasons why you *can* achieve it. These are your "I CAN!" statements.

Those statements might be:

- I can buy a house.
- I can buy a car.
- I can have a relationship.
- I can travel the world.
- I can have residual income.

- I can exist.
- I can is real.
- I can make $1,000,000.
- I can retire young.
- I can travel the world.
- I can go to the gym.
- I can run a mile in less than five minutes.
- I can do it!

Once you've completed writing all your "I CAN!" statements, burn the first sheet containing the negative statements. Following this advice from my mentor has proven effective for me, and I can attest that it works!

While acknowledging that some of the tasks you list in your affirmations may be challenging, remember that with determination, you can accomplish those goals. I know, because I did it!

Chapter 7 Study Questions

1. "What you see is what you get." Explain this statement in terms of your success in achieving your goal.

_____

_____

_____

_____

_____

2. This exercise has two parts. First: write down the things you see in your life or situation that you don't like.

_____

_____

_____

_____

_____

3. Second: now write down the things you see in your life that you do like. When you are done, cross out the list above.

_____

_____

_____

_____

_____

4. Get two pieces of paper and go through the **positive** and **negative** beliefs exercise from this chapter. Write about how you feel after burning the first page.

_____

_____

_____

_____

_____

Chapter 8

"I CAN'T" DOES EXIST

You might be asking, "The title of this book is *I Can't Doesn't Exist*. So why now say that it does?" It's a valid question, and the explanation is here if you read on!

This chapter is set to be quite intriguing as I open up about personal aspects of my life that you may not know about.

As I write this book, I find myself at 40, anticipating my 41st year. I can vividly remember being a 15-year-old, roaming the streets of Chicago with friends who weren't the best influences. I wasn't much better myself, allowing their negative mindset to shape the way I thought. In return, I got bad results. I didn't know it at the time, but those negative results were happening by law; I was focusing my attention on negative places.

Then something terrible happened.

One of my friends was shot in Chicago. Worried about my safety, my parents took action. They sent me to Houston, Texas, to live with my uncle's family and continue my education. They feared I might meet the same fate as my friend if I stayed in Chicago with the wrong crowd.

These are the kinds of challenges life threw at me, shaping the person I am today.

A lot of failures that, in the end, led to my success.

Now, let's revisit the stories of Henry Ford and Thomas Edison. Both of these visionaries encountered thousands of failures on their journeys. Edison's relentless pursuit of innovation resulted in thousands of failures before finally creating the incandescent lightbulb. Similarly, Henry Ford faced numerous setbacks yet persevered through thousands of failures, ultimately resulting in the Ford Model T and later the V8 engine.

These great men faced criticism and resistance because their ideas were unprecedented. However, they went on to revolutionize the modern world.

Today, we take for granted the presence of electricity in our homes, with the convenience of walking into a well-lit house when it's dark outside. And beyond the walls of our homes, the cityscape is also illuminated at night.

During the time I roamed the streets of my neighborhood, I went through many failures. Internally, I wished it was different, but as just a kid, I just didn't know what else to do.

Even as the years passed, finding the right mentor, a true leader, proved challenging. Sometimes mentors fail you. In my younger days, I found a misguided mentor who indeed led me down the wrong path. I learned to be careful about whom to follow.

Eventually, I returned to Chicago from Houston with a determination to change my life. I chose not to spend too much time with people engaging in house parties and drinking at a young age. I would join them at times, but my focus was on searching for truth—a task as difficult as finding a needle in a haystack. However, I sensed there was more to discover, something I was missing.

In 2010, I faced what I thought was another failure when I was arrested by the police for driving drunk. Another failure! Like I said, there have been many failures on my journey.

I had to do something different. I moved into my mom's basement and delved into personal development, reading *Think and Grow Rich* by Napoleon Hill and scouring You-Tube for videos on the subject. One memorable discovery was an old 1980s video featuring Bob Proctor, a young white man in a brown suit with big glasses. His words resonated with me. It felt like he knew I would be out there in the future, seeking the truth. Every word he spoke made me feel like I had found my mentor.

I continued to immerse myself in Bob Proctor's lectures and Napoleon Hill's writings. The turning point came when I had the opportunity to meet Bob Proctor in person. By then, I was already absorbed in studying his book *You Were Born Rich* and listening to his seminars daily. As I embraced the teachings, I learned to think and act with a clear goal in mind. Keeping a journal, I wrote down my thoughts and actions. I had started to create the life I wanted.

When I look back at some of my older journals, before I found the information from Bob Proctor, all of my writing centered on the things I didn't want. It was all negative. For example, I would write, "It's going to be hard for me to graduate college. I flunked mathematics. No good in math. So, I'm possibly not going to graduate." It was a cycle of negativity.

However, fueled by courage and faith, I made the decision to return to school in 2008, before my son was born. I pursued a Finance and Investment Management degree at Northwestern College, with aspirations to work for JP Morgan or Goldman Sachs. Eventually, in 2010, I secured a position at JP Morgan Chase.

Unfortunately, the DUI arrest in 2010 altered my course. I had to resign from my job due to a sentence that required completion of Army boot camp.

All these apparent failures turned out to be a blessing. They guided me to Napoleon Hill, my mentor, even though he had long been dead. Studying Napoleon Hill's principles through the teachings of Bob Proctor changed the way I thought and, consequently, my life.

You have the potential to do the same through this book, *I Can't Doesn't Exist*, but it's up to you and what you choose to say. Just as it was for me. The words I once penned in my early journals weren't serving me well. Now my journals say:

- I'm so happy and grateful now!
- I'm healthy, I'm happy, and I'm wealthy.
- I've earned more than $140 million.
- I'm traveling the world.
- I have a house on the beach.
- I live in Europe and have a house in Tulum.
- I travel to the United States whenever my heart desires.
- I have multiple streams of income.
- I have a beautiful wife.
- I have a beautiful family.
- I love my son.
- I have great parents.
- I have good friendships.

This is the mentality you need to have.

Begin by examining your past. Where have you focused your attention—your thoughts, actions, and desires? This process will let you discover all the ways you've been saying, "I can't," and you'll become more aware of your thoughts. You can find a new path, and this book is designed to guide you on the new journey. It empowers you to change your life by envisioning the life you truly desire and declaring confidently, "I CAN!"

Chapter 8 Study Questions

1. As I did, write about the time in your life when you realized there must be another way to achieve success.

_____

_____

_____

_____

_____

2. Who is responsible for the world you live in? What CAN you do about it to make a change?

_____

_____

_____

_____

_____

3. Make a list of the things you are grateful for in your life. Use your journal, so you can come back and read it again.

_____

_____

_____

_____

_____

4. Write a list of your reasons for saying, "I can't." Then, write a positive version of that list starting with "I can!"

_____

_____

_____

_____

_____

Chapter 9

DREAMING

Y ou can!

This ties back to our earlier discussion about a crucial aspect—your imagination.

Recall how I talked about the God-given abilities, your higher faculties:

- Imagination
- Will
- Reason
- Intuition
- Memory
- Perception

This is your toolbox for creating the world of your dreams. This toolbox is equipped with everything you need to be successful beyond your wildest dreams. The sole obstacle in your path is yourself, so dare to dream that you can.

Genevieve Behrend's insight resonates powerfully. She says that bringing these unseen realities into harmony with your conception enables you to transform seemingly fantastic dreams into practical working realities.

Your conception is essentially your thought. All things begin in the mind before turning into physical reality.

The key lies in aligning these unseen causes with your conception. By doing so, you can transform fantastical dreams into practical working realities.

The phrase "practical working realities" means that multiple realities coexist—the world of dreams and the real world. The subconscious mind doesn't know the difference between the two. It gives you what you focus your attention on, influenced also by your prevailing vibrations.

If your desired goal encounters difficulties in materializing, it's because you haven't fit all the right pieces together, like solving a puzzle.

That's what this book is for.

This book serves the purpose of helping you understand that there's a connection missing between your conscious and subconscious mind. Something is hindering the realization of your fantasy, your dream.

As Genevieve Behrend suggests, it's about transforming present dreams into practical working realities.

Maybe at this point you feel awesome, ready and excited to make your first move. The excitement of exploring the world might be on your mind, whether it's the baby blue waters of Cancun, the enchanting Bahamas, the mystique of Egypt's pyramids, the grandeur of Rome's Colosseum, or perhaps checking off the Seven Wonders of the World.

Everything becomes possible through this information because, remember, the subconscious mind doesn't differentiate between a penny and $1,000,000. It's amenable to suggestion. So, the more you focus your thoughts on what you want, affirming, "I can do this," the subconscious mind will bring down the brick wall that's standing in your way.

It'll tear down the wall and say, "Alright, come on in. Let me give you what you want because you've been pushing on that wall for so long. You've pushed through so many failures, so dream that you can."

As Genevieve Behrend and I have both said, the dream world is just as real as the waking world. They coexist. A lucid dream holds the same reality as the experiences in this waking dimension. That dream world is also a dimension in itself.

There are infinite frequencies. There are infinite dimensions. There are infinite places you can explore.

Do you want to go on a helicopter flight? Well, here's a revelation: as you read about it in this book, you've already soared through the skies in your imagination. You can go anywhere you want.

I want you to choose your own path. While I have the ability to take you on diverse journeys, you don't have to follow me; you can go where you really want to go. Consider this a lesson: find a tranquil space, whether it's your room or another quiet place, and write:

- Where are you now?
- Where do you want to go? (be specific and detailed)
- How do you feel now that you've arrived at this place that you've been searching for?
- How do you feel now that you've made it?
- How do you feel now that they just rolled out the red carpet for you?

Imagine this: You're in a place of your dreams. They're saying your name and taking your photo. They're saying, "Hey, we want your autograph!"

"Why? Why do you want my autograph?"

"Because you created this. You built a company that made a significant impact and changed people's lives. Yes, you! It's all because of you. How do you feel? We want to ask you questions!"

And you. You have silence before you speak. There's a moment of nervousness, but then you let it all out, saying, "I feel great! I'm so happy I did it. It was tough at the beginning, you know? I faced numerous failures while trying to build my company. I struggled to find the right people for the job, but then I met this other person, and suddenly, 'I can't' transformed into 'I can.' Because energy is intelligent, much like gravity putting everything in its proper order."

This energy reaches out to people, conversing with them in silence, in the space. It's telling me, "Hey, this person needs help. I want you to meet him at 9:00 at a coffee shop on this specific date." The person isn't aware.

No one is really aware of it because this energy is something invisible, like an aura.

In 1930s, a photographer named Semyon Kirlian perfected Kirlian photography, a technique capturing the aura leaving someone's body and radiating. It's like an energy field.

We are constantly attracting one aura while repelling another, broadcasting signals like a TV station. You receive a signal and you let another signal go. Guess what? This energy communicates with like-minded people to help manifest your dreams.

Dream boldly and bring these people into your life by writing down your goals. Write down what you want, and stay focused. Better yet, envision how you'd feel once you've made it—once you've achieved your dreams. Create a goal card or a piece of paper detailing everything you've accomplished, starting from the end, from the perspective of having already achieved your goal.

Think FROM the feeling of the goal achieved rather than thinking OF the goal itself.

Begin not from ABCD but from Z, working your way backward in time to the present NOW. How does it feel knowing that you've made it?

Now, enter into meditation. Find a quiet space, and begin to write down all those feelings. Describe how incredible you feel!

Chapter 9 Study Questions

1. Write down four of the higher faculties in your tool-box. From your own understanding, tell how each one can help you succeed.

_____

_____

_____

_____

_____

2. Describe what Genevieve Behrend said on how can thoughts be changed into practical working reality?

_____

_____

_____

_____

_____

3. Your thoughts of success are your goal statement. Write your goal statement again, with details and strong emotion.

_____

_____

_____

_____

_____

4. Imagine that you have achieved the life of your
    dreams. Write how people around you react to the
    new, changed YOU.

    _____

    _____

    _____

    _____

    _____

Chapter 10

PARADIGMS DESTROY
"I CAN!"

So, what are paradigms? Paradigms are habits of thinking. They're the thoughts you've heard repeatedly since childhood, from parents, siblings, friends, and teachers. Often, they are thoughts of "I can't," though we now understand that "I can't" doesn't truly exist.

Even if a thought isn't true, hearing it repeatedly can make you believe it is true, and it becomes your reality. If someone tells you "You're not good at math," you might not initially believe it, but with repetition from different sources, it starts to affect your perception. The more you hear it from others, the more you might start to believe, "I'm not good at math." You begin to internalize the idea, repeating it until it becomes your belief. This happened to me.

Let's talk about what I experienced at age 15. Being Hispanic in the United States often means being perceived merely as a statistic. Expectations were low; the assumption was that I wouldn't wear nice clothes in college or work for a bank. Instead, I was supposed to end up flipping burgers at McDonald's or delivering milk for Starbucks—jobs I eventually took on. I worked at McDonald's, and later at Circuit City, before transitioning to Starbucks to deliver milk.

I didn't particularly enjoy those jobs, but why did I take them? It was all for the money. That's why I often say, "Don't do things for money!" Follow your passion, and the money will come. Let me repeat it: Do what you love, and the money will come.

Take a moment to reflect: Are you currently doing what you love? Stop and ask yourself, "Why am I doing this job?"

You might say, "Because I have kids." Or…

- "Because I have a mortgage payment."
- "Because I have a house."
- "Because I have bills to pay."

And that's perfectly fine if your reasons are coming from a spirit of gratitude. Remind yourself, "I'm so happy and grateful for my house, my family, my kids, and my job," especially considering that many people don't have jobs, and some are living beneath bridges.

Take a closer look at your life. Identify habits that aren't propelling you to the next level, preventing you from becoming the person living the life you truly love.

Maybe you have too much time on your hands, or perhaps you lack sufficient hunger for something better. You might aspire to make $1,000,000 or start a company, but concerns about the "how" could be hindering you. There are countless "maybes" that might block your path.

However, I'm here to tell you that you don't need to know how. You don't need every detail or every next step. What you need to know is "I can!" and recognize that "I can't" is a concept that doesn't exist.

Because these thoughts that hinder you are paradigms. They act as self-imposed roadblocks. Remember, what is a paradigm? It's a habitual way of thinking, a thinking habit.

Paradigms are programs that you've seen or heard and information that you've absorbed from others. They wield control over everything in your life—your income, your love life, your success, every aspect of your life.

A paradigm keeps you stuck in the same place, creating a sense of paralysis, much like a drug addict stuck in the same patterns. It takes you backwards, feeding you lies and false reasons why you can't.

But the truth is, you can!

You can, thanks to the law of polarity. In every situation, there's a balance of negative and positive forces. By consistently maintaining positive thoughts, as emphasized by Wallace Wattles in *The Science of Getting Rich*, you will attract whatever you desire through the law of polarity and gender.

In life, there are 24 hours in a day, 365 days in a year, and 4 distinct seasons. We don't experience two seasons simultaneously. When you earnestly write down your goal, believe in it, sign and date it, you set in motion a magnetic force that is going to attract your desire on the specified date.

It happened to me. It happened to Bob Proctor. It happened to John Canary, Bob Proctor's partner. It also happened to Jack Canfield, the author of *Chicken Soup for the Soul*. Despite initial skepticism from others, Jack Canfield not only sold 50 million copies of his book but also went on to sell the company for millions of dollars.

"I can't" only exists if you grant it belief. The key is to believe in yourself first and foremost. Stop listening to the limiting paradigms that insist, "I can't," and instead, start telling the truth.

Begin affirming, "I can!" until it resonates as your undeniable truth.

This book aims to guide you in understanding that multiple realities coexist. You may be living in one dimension, but it has the potential to open your awareness to all the possibilities across different dimensions. This shift allows you to tap into new potentials and accelerate your progress, making what is known as a quantum leap from one level to another effortlessly—provided you change your perspective.

Recognize that you operate on an energetic level called a vibration—a frequency of attraction stemming from the energy of your thoughts. If your vibrations are off, if your heart isn't in it, if doubt clouds your belief in your capabilities, you hinder your ability to attain what you truly desire.

That's why engaging in activities you enjoy, like going to the gym, is crucial. Undertaking productive and enjoyable activities allows you to take control of your paradigm, aligning yourself with the vibration of what you truly desire in your life.

Creating a new paradigm involves the third level, the third way to generate income. Let's delve into these levels:

Level 1: Involves a job where you exchange time for money, receiving either an hourly wage or a salary. This is like my experiences at McDonald's or at Chase.

Level 2: Involves trading money for more money. This is when you put your money to work. Investors make money by having their capital earn interest, increase in value through stocks, or grow in some other way.

Level 3: Transforming ideas into money. The energy of thoughts can be altered or transformed, manifesting money seemingly out of thin air. Although it may sound impossible, money is simply another form of energy and follows all the same laws of nature. Similar to water existing in various states—solid as an iceberg, liquid as the ocean, or invisible vapor as air—money can also take different forms. If you burn the air, it turns into ether. It's in the etheric realm.

That's like God-level. This is what energy is all about. In our universe, there's more nonphysical matter than physical matter. Almost all of the energy in the universe is like this; it can't be seen or measured, but it's still there.

As Wallace Wattles said, "There's a thinking stuff from which all things are made. A thought impressed upon this stuff produces the thing that's imaged by the thought."

There's a dynamic at play in the unseen part of the universe, and the key is to tap into the unseen so you can create the life you want. Your paradigms, the ingrained thoughts within you, may have previously dictated "I can't," but through the creation of new paradigms, you can shape a world aligned with your highest dreams.

So, what can you do?

Start by analyzing your thoughts. Listen to what you're thinking in your mind. If the thoughts originate from your paradigm, saying, "I can't," just counteract them by affirming "I CAN!" in your mind.

Before long, you will start to understand:

- that all realities exist
- that you're going to create your own reality
- that you're going to take control of the paradigm
- that you're going to take control of your feelings, not someone else
- that no one can control how you feel

Only you have control over how you feel because only you can govern the images and thoughts that traverse your mind throughout the day. These thoughts seamlessly enter your subconscious mind, which is wide open, eagerly awaiting suggestions. It's like the subconscious mind is saying, "Tell me what you're thinking about, and I will give it to you."

If you repeatedly tell yourself, "I can't buy a car," "I can't buy a house," "I can't focus," or "I can't create anything," you solidify the belief in your mind that you indeed can't. Your thoughts become your reality, echoing the fundamental principle that:

"I can't" doesn't exist. "I can't" doesn't exist!

If that's true, then what does exist? Your thoughts exist.

You might ask questions like, "How can 'you can' exist?" "If my thought isn't real, how can it exist?"

Consider this: "If it's in my mind, how did Leonardo da Vinci create the Mona Lisa?" He created the Mona Lisa in his mind, and the masterpiece displayed in the Louvre Museum in Paris is a replica, a second copy. The original, the first copy, existed solely in da Vinci's mind, and he took it with him when he passed away.

Your life is a copy of your thoughts. You are the sum total of all that you've thought about—past, present, and future!

Think about that.

Reflect on your current situation. Then, envision where you want to be, and ponder why you might have been holding yourself back. Negative paradigms have the potential to be destructive, but the power of positive paradigms can obliterate the "I can't" mindset. Positive paradigms played a transformative role in dismantling the "I can't" mentality in my own life.

You have the power to transform your life, reshaping the paradigm of "I can't." You can craft a new paradigm that steers your life toward abundance, steering clear of poverty, misery, wants, and needs.

Remember, I mentioned that friend who said to me, "I want to buy a car." Such expressions often come from a place of necessity.

Yet, it's crucial to remember this: You don't actually *need* anything. As Bob Proctor has emphasized, you were born rich.

You are wealthy.

You are happy.

You are healthy.

You are a creator.

You are a very smart person.

Make your visions, your dreams, a reality!

Chapter 10 Study Questions

1. Paradigms are habitual ways of thinking. Explain how they can shape your world, both in terms of success and failure.

    _____

    _____

    _____

    _____

    _____

2. Money is energy exchanged for value. What are the three levels of exchange? What level are you on now? Where do you want to be?

    _____

    _____

    _____

    _____

    _____

3. What four things do you need to know in order to reach your goal, in addition to writing your goal card?

    _____

    _____

    _____

    _____

    _____

4. Make a list of "I can!" statements that affirm your
   positive paradigms. Read the list aloud to yourself and
   memorize it.

   _____

   _____

   _____

   _____

   _____

Chapter 11

EVERYTHING IS

Make your visions and dreams a reality!

How do you do that?

You do that by understanding the laws.

You do that by understanding that nothing is created, and nothing is destroyed. Everything you desire already exists.

Science and theology disagree on a lot of things, but they come together on one point: nothing is created, and nothing is destroyed. This implies that the life you desire already exists, even if it's imperceptible to your senses. It resides on a specific frequency, in a particular dimension.

What you must do is build a more empowering image of "I can," a more compelling image of "I already did," and a more vivid image of "Everything's already here, and I'm tapping into it right now!"

Bring it into reality. Visit the Gucci store. Step into the dealership of the car you desire. Immerse yourself in luxury because luxury is within your grasp—everything is within your grasp.

God didn't intend for you to be broke. God's intention is for you to experience the best that life has to offer. Society may have suggested otherwise, enforcing the notion that "Who you are is a worker who works nine to five." But you have the power to change that narrative that tells you, "You work hard but never get ahead. That's who you are, and it will never change. Get over it, and get to work."

Let me tell you who you truly are. You are a spirit, God's highest form of creation. God did not design you to beg; God intended for you to prosper and achieve success.

Because you carry the God particle, the spirit of God living inside you and with you, you have the power to create anything you desire. You are a part of Him, and He is a part of you.

You can create anything you want! Engage your imagination and ask yourself, "How do I feel now that I have this life of my dreams?"

I manifested my visions into reality. I now own a beautiful house in Portugal, one in Marbella, Spain, and others in

Cancun and Tulum. I travel between the United States and Europe, have friends around the world.

Some of my friends were left behind because they couldn't comprehend that "I can't" doesn't exist. Their negativity, as I mentioned earlier, tried to hold me back. They only understood their limitations and projected them onto me, staying in a stagnant place, content with nothing. Their mindset was one of complacency, settling for a job, thinking, "Yeah, it's okay. I'm okay having this job because, by the time I'm 65, I'll have a pension, live off it, and be fine because I have insurance."

It's not that there's anything wrong with that approach, but the essence of this book is about transcending to the next level—just as I did when I became a multi-millionaire, having enough money to buy three properties in a month, purchase a Ferrari in cash, and buy a Mercedes G-Wagon.

Is it real? Yes, it's real.

As Genevieve Behrend aptly states, "Oh, fantastic dream!" You have the potential to live a fantastic dream through your fantasies, but there are things you need to understand.

The truth is, you've been programmed. Just like the paradigms instilled in you from a young age—put away the crayons, go to school, pay attention, do as you're told, and work to achieve A's and B's. Guess what? Thomas Edison might have had numerous F's as a kid, leading to his expulsion. However, he went on to become a genius, one of the greatest minds of all time.

I faced a string of C's, D's, and F's, sprinkled with a few A's and B's. Then it happened. I made a poor decision, driving drunk and receiving a DUI, resulting in the loss of his job at the bank. But was his life over? Far from it! It was just the beginning of a new life. I went on to create my own reality, amassing millions of dollars in the process!

Here's a task for you. Ask yourself, "Who are you?" Take a moment to look in the mirror, much like Napoleon Hill did when Andrew Carnegie urged him to do the same and recite certain affirmations.

Consider this another lesson, another chapter in this book. The title is "My Life." Before concluding this chapter and the book itself, undertake this exercise for the future YOU.

Go ahead, look in the mirror. Tell yourself, "I AM the person who…" and complete that sentence by vividly describing the life of your dreams. Make it a daily practice. Return to the mirror, and tell yourself about the person you are becoming. Write down this future dream life that you love. Stand in front of the mirror before going to sleep and affirm it to yourself.

Read aloud what you've written. This becomes your script, your life script, defining who you are. "My name is _____. I'm going to sell 50 million books like Jack Canfield. I'm a New York Times bestselling author. I'm happy and grateful that I'm traveling the world."

You have the power to attain anything you want—unlimited, with no restrictions.

It's akin to a magician pulling a rabbit out of a hat. Perhaps it's because everyone wanted to see the rabbit.

What do you want to pull out of that magician's hat?

- Do you want to pull out a new house?

- Do you want to pull out a car?

- Do you want to pull out your girlfriend, wife, or fiancé?

- Do you want to pull out a private jet?

- Do you want to pull out an experience, perhaps going to London and marveling at Big Ben?

- Do you want to go to Egypt?

- Would you like to travel to Chicago and visit Navy Pier?

- Would you like to go to the Statue of Liberty in New York or bask on the sunny beaches of Miami?

- Would you like to visit San Francisco and gaze at the Golden Gate Bridge?

- Would you like to explore Chinatown in San Francisco?

- How about a trip to the Bahamas, Puerto Rico, Spain, Germany, or Japan?

The possibilities are limitless—you can go wherever you want!

I've lived through these experiences, but it all started with a realization. I told myself, "I'm tired of getting the same results. I want something different."

My poor choices and a distorted self-image nearly led to a tragic incident.

Because I made the choice to drink and drive, I found myself in jail, ultimately losing my job at the bank. I wouldn't wish anyone to go through the challenges I faced, and that's why I began writing books.

I realized that my personal experiences and journey held a story with a moral—a tale I could share with others. Has it been easy? No! There have been numerous failures along my path, and you will likely face failures too, just like me, Thomas Edison, and my mentor, Bob Proctor.

Bob often spoke about the razor's edge—the thin line between success and failure. It's a delicate balance, dependent on your perspective. That's the polarity—positive and negative. Which side are you looking at, the positive or the negative?

It's a narrow razor's edge, so reflect on that. Think about the challenges I faced. Consider what you're currently going through, and empower yourself by reading this book. Repetition is crucial, like learning to throw a baseball—practice it at least a thousand times.

This is how you change the paradigm. A paradigm clings to the habits you've learned, insisting you need to keep working, that you can't do it. If you believe this, you tell yourself, "I can't do it."

When everyone around you says, "You can't do it," and you give up, saying, "I can't do it," that's when you've failed. But I am here to assert that you can do it, that "I can't" doesn't exist. You can be whatever you want to be. Just remember what I told you, "You can do it!" Even if you don't believe in yourself, believe that I believe in you.

I've been there, and now I live in the world of my dreams. Not because I'm special—I'm not. But I discovered the power of not listening to the negative paradigm. Instead, I listened to the best mentors and learned to transform my thinking.

It's all in your mind. Take a journey there, to the realm of fantasy, just as Genevieve Behrend suggests—to the fantastic dream, and construct images of abundance.

Build images of:

- I'm not going to worry about how much this suit is going to cost me.
- I'm not going to worry about the cost of groceries to feed my family and myself.
- I'm not going to worry about my gym membership fee.

"Like a river flows and keeps on flowing, there's more money coming in. I can spend whatever I want."

I recall going to Canada on a work trip with Bob Proctor. Bob was on stage saying, "I've never looked at a receipt when I went to the store, to the grocery store, or when I bought a suit. I can't remember the day when I would look at a receipt."

You may hear that and say, "That's impossible." But it happens to me all the time now. For example, when I went to a nice restaurant in London with my son. He was in shock at the price of our bill. We went to the finest restaurant in London and ordered the finest meat—Wagyu beef. The bill was $1500, and yes, I enjoyed a bottle of wine with an associate of mine, one of my students from London.

My son was in shock because he had never eaten Wagyu beef before. The tenderness and flavor were unimaginably excellent—of the highest quality, perfect. He told me,

"What a difference it is eating at this restaurant compared to a regular steakhouse." Your life can be like this, too!

Increase the things that you want. Ask for the best. Expand your goals. Increase the amount of money you want to make. Because nothing is created, and nothing is destroyed.

Everything you want is already here.

You just need to tap into it. You just need a bit of a push. Read this book 100 times. 1000 times! Just like I did, listening to and reading Napoleon Hill. I have read his words at least 1000 times.

This was what Bob Procter did and how Edison worked to invent the incandescent light. You need to do the same thing.

If you do, you will finally take the quantum leap that will propel you with rocket force to another level. To look back to the place you started from, you will need a telescope, as Bob Proctor used to say. And now I can agree with all my heart, "Bob was right." Likewise, if you follow the lessons I've explained in this book, one day, you will look back and say, "Ross was right."

You don't always need to check the receipt. Go into situations with the mindset that you can have anything you want, that you can do anything you want, and that "I can" does exist.

You can break the paradigm. You can change your life by reading a book and applying the lessons therein. This is what personal growth and development are all about, and these are the lessons I've been implementing in my life since 2010. I've studied the information and grown beyond what I ever imagined.

Remember:

You must create your own visions of reality and fall in love with them. Never, never, never give up. Know deep within your heart that "I can't" doesn't exist. Tell yourself, "I can. I Can! I CAN!!"

Chapter 11 Study Questions

1. "Nothing is created, and nothing is destroyed." What does this mean? How can this help you achieve your desires?

    _____

    _____

    _____

    _____

    _____

2. You have within you the character of God. What are some of the qualities of this character? What can you do that God also does?

    _____

    _____

    _____

    _____

    _____

3. Look in the mirror and tell yourself: "I AM the person who…" Finish the sentence below. Read it aloud every day.

    _____

    _____

    _____

    _____

    _____

4. Write your goal statement again. Remember what you have just read. Ask largely. Ask for the best. All things are possible!

_____

_____

_____

_____

_____

CONCLUSION

This book has taken a long time to write. It has taken my entire life up to this point, including my mistakes, failures, and successes.

I've shared a portion of my life story, detailing my journey from being on the wrong track and on the wrong side of the law to becoming a happy and successful multi-millionaire.

Yet, there are three crucial points that I want to emphasize once again.

FIRST

If you don't like the course of life you're on, take this step: Walk into your bathroom, and look at yourself in the mirror. In that reflection, you'll see the only person responsible for the life you're currently living—you'll see yourself.

Speak these words to your reflection: "I am responsible for my life. I accept my responsibility. I forgive myself for every mistake I've made. I recognize that all possibilities exist, and I CAN become a new person. I AM a new person who embraces abundance, success, and living the best life!"

Practice this exercise until it becomes ingrained. Utter these words aloud, and imagine you actually ARE the person you aspire to be in the future. Fall in love with that person and with the life you dream of.

SECOND

Saying "I CAN!" marks just the first step. You have to actually DO something. Develop a plan and get started; take that FIRST STEP. It can be a small step, but the first step is crucial. Take ACTION with INTENTION. When you take the first step, visualize yourself already immersed in the life of your dreams. Behave as if you've already reached the success you want. Behave like a multi-millionaire. This is your intent. Begin to think and act as if you've already arrived. Embody this newfound persona in everything you do. Cultivate habits that align with success.

THIRD

Focus your attention on the exhilarating feeling of being a success! You radiate amazement, gratitude, benevolence, joy, inspiration, and fulfillment. Nothing can stand in your way! The power of heightened emotion is

HUGE. Emotion propels your new life closer to you. Relax, and allow the Infinite to advance toward you. Focus your emotions and anticipation toward your new life, your prosperous future of success, wealth, and all the finest aspects of life.

Remember that your thoughts wield unparalleled influence in all of creation. Maintain unwavering focus on your dream, envisioning yourself as the successful person of your highest imagination. Approach every action from the perspective that your new life is already a reality. You deserve the very best, and you are entitled to the life you dream of. You will BE the person you spend your time thinking about.

It's all up to you now. Pay no attention to those who say you can't. Pay no attention to the things beyond your control or that are negative. Revisit this book, and revisit the study questions. Repeat your goals aloud, in front of a mirror. Carry your goal card, and reflect upon it with joy. Watch for signals guiding you to the next step. Enjoy the process!

October 11th 2019 Paradigm Shift Event
Hilton LAX California
Ross Garcia and Price Pritchett

ABOUT THE AUTHOR

Ross Garcia is living proof that the Law of Attraction works.

As a boy, Ross moved from Houston, Texas, to Chicago. His father was a hard-working construction man who brought home barely enough money to feed the family, which included his wife, Ross, and two other children.

An average American child, Ross was interested in martial arts, skateboarding, and collecting sports cards. He would often play in the streets near his home or in the local park, where he and his friends could get a free lunch.

When he turned fifteen, changes started to take place, based on decisions Ross was making. He was hanging out with the wrong crowd. His dad made the tough decision to send him back to Houston to live with his uncle. These were the early days of gang violence.

After a year, Ross moved back to Chicago, where he finished high school. He found a fast-food job, moved into retail tool sales, and eventually into selling cell phones. Doors were opening, but Ross felt that there was something more to his life than working hard. He was searching for himself.

While waiting at a bus stop, an idea came to him. Ross remembered words of advice, "Go to school. Get a degree."

Ross wanted to go to college, but was met with failure when he discovered his math skills didn't make the cut. He studied hard to improve and was admitted to college, earning a degree in finance.

Then his life took a sudden detour.

Driving drunk, Ross caused a serious car accident. He was sentenced to four months in a disciplinary boot camp, which changed his perspective. There, Ross started reading Napoleon Hill's *Think and Grow Rich*. Hill taught about having a burning desire, a goal, and that money was just a form of energy. When his four months at boot camp were finished, Ross was looking for a way to make money.

His friend told him about his job at the bank, writing mort- gages, and Ross soon found himself in the same position. He was making money. Napoleon Hill said to find something you're good at and get better at it. Ross was good at restruc- turing mortgages, and he got better. He made more money, and in so doing he helped people keep their homes. Hill had written about being on the right side. Ross was there.

Ross studied Napoleon Hill daily, learning about the importance of writing down goals. Ross wrote down his goal: to make $1.75 million within five years. He had no idea how he would do that. But it started him thinking.

About halfway through those five years, Ross met Bob Proctor, who also studied Napoleon Hill. Bob offered a consultant training program, and Ross signed up. He knew that having Bob as a coach would help him, but he also knew that all the answers he needed were already inside him. The path from where you are to where you want to be is never the path you expect.

Just as the five years came to a close, Ross had made $1.75 million. His goal was accomplished, just like Napoleon Hill said it would happen. So, Ross set a new goal.

He wanted to be rich. Not so much just to be *rich*, but he knew if he was a consultant telling people how to succeed, he needed to be an example. He needed to succeed himself. He told himself about the life he would live. "I'm a writer. I give lectures. I'm not worried about money, because I have more than enough. I'm helping people do what I do—succeed. I make $50 million in cryptocurrency!"

"Anything is possible. I have a house in front of the ocean, and I get all my money from my earnings in cryptocurrency." His mortgage business was doing well, so he decided to start investing in crypto. Soon, he started making more money.

Reading became the one thing Ross did more and more of. He had a burning desire to succeed, and he read the writ- ings of others who had done the same thing. He started traveling. His travels took him to Switzerland, the UK, and Spain. His mortgage restructuring prospered, and so did his crypto investments.

By the time another five years had passed, Ross had exceeded his $50 million goal.

Ross now holds a passport from Portugal, has a house in front of the ocean in Marbella, a second home in Tulum, and travels often between Europe and the Americas. He writes, lectures, consults, and runs sev- eral businesses including CryptoLifeSchool.com and wealthmindsetgroup.com

Anything is possible! Ross Garcia is proof.

AVAILABLE NOW ON AMAZON.

FOR MORE INFO ABOUT
I CAN'T DOESN'T EXISTG
UPCOMING BOOKS
OR ROSS GARCIA,

VISIT

www.ROSSGARCIAAUTHOR.COM

MORE BOOKS COMING SOON...

www.ingramcontent.com/pod-product-compliance
Lightning Source LLC
Chambersburg PA
CBHW060612200326
41521CB00007B/758